Home Office Research Study 234

Empowering young people in rural Suffolk

An evaluation report for the Home Office

Women's Policy Research Unit
University of East Anglia

The views expressed in this report are those of the authors, not necessarily those of the Home Office (nor do they reflect Government policy).

Home Office Research, Development and Statistics Directorate
December 2001

Home Office Research Studies

The Home Office Research Studies are reports on research undertaken by or on behalf of the Home Office. They cover the range of subjects for which the Home Secretary has responsibility. Other publications produced by the Research, Development and Statistics Directorate include Findings, Statistical Bulletins and Statistical Papers.

The Research, Development and Statistics Directorate

RDS is part of the Home Office. The Home Office's purpose is to build a safe, just and tolerant society in which the rights and responsibilities of individuals, families and communities are properly balanced and the protection and security of the public are maintained.

RDS is also part of National Statistics (NS). One of the aims of NS is to inform Parliament and the citizen about the state of the nation and provide a window on the work and performance of government, allowing the impact of government policies and actions to be assessed.

Therefore –

Research Development and Statistics Directorate exists to improve policy making, decision taking and practice in support of the Home Office purpose and aims, to provide the public and Parliament with information necessary for informed debate and to publish information for future use.

First published 2001
Application for reproduction should be made to the Communication Development Unit, Room 201, Home Office, 50 Queen Anne's Gate, London SW1H 9AT.
© Crown copyright 2001   ISBN 1 84082 778 5
                            ISSN 0072 6435

Foreword

This paper is one of a group of development reports about projects funded by the Home Office Programme Development Unit (PDU), part of the Research Development and Statistics Directorate. The Programme Development Unit existed from 1992 – 2000; it was set up specifically to encourage, fund and develop innovative local projects about issues related to crime and criminal justice. The Unitt's objective was to try to build a bridge between pure research and practice. Two cycles of funding were made available: 1992-1995 and 1996-1999.

Evaluation reports for the five projects funded in the second phase[1], including this one, are being published in the HORS series. Also being published to coincide with these reports are a small number of evaluation reports[2] from the first phase of work, which involved extremely experimental approaches both to development and to evaluation. These are being published as Occasional Papers.

All of these reports relate to early intervention initiatives directed at providing support to children who were, as a rule, not offenders but whose lives include a number of the circumstances which have been identified as risk factors for offending. Interventions range from work with young primary school children to initiatives with excluded secondary school pupils and first-time offenders and, as in this report, with young people who may be experiencing social exclusion as a result of particular circumstances.

The PDU programme was extremely developmental, and evaluators were specifically tasked to consider not only the outcomes of the projects (which in many cases, because of the nature of the interventions and the ages of the participants, can only be early or intermediate outcomes), but also to look carefully at the process of development and implementation and to include a substantial core of descriptive material about the participants and their circumstances. The reports provide a great deal of useful material about the characteristics of the young people involved and their families. They also describe the ways in which agencies responsible for interventions relate to their clients and to each other; discuss the practicality and success of interventions themselves and analyse early indicators of success or failure. All of this knowledge is especially relevant to the many new initiatives either under way or

---

1   Project CHANCE
     Meeting Need and Challenging Crime in Partnership with Schools
     Dalston Youth Project
     Youth Crime Reduction Project
2   The Dorset Healthy Alliance Project
     The Sheffield C'mon Everybody Project

planned, including the Children and Young Persons' Unit programmes and New Deal For Communities, together with much other national and local crime reduction work. Although the degree of evaluative rigour varies, these reports nonetheless contain valuable and constructive learning about why, for whom, and how intervention should be planned.

This report describes a challenging attempt to work in a structural and structured way with small groups of young people in a number of very rural locations. The original aims and principles of the project were ambitious and the evaluators have recorded the difficulties of converting the concepts of empowerment and involvement into practical action.

Throughout the project, the rurality of the area generated its own complications. Rurality – particularly the problems which affect communication – has an impact on practice and also on attitudes. The project area was extensive and, as the evaluators note, public transportation was rare or non-existent for most of it. Distance played a significant part in determining how and when young people could be contacted and interventions delivered; it also had an impact on the advisory group because of the difficulty of scheduling meetings with agency members whose areas of responsibility covered many miles and for whom meetings involved several hours' commitment.

The project achieved some significant success in motivating both young people and adults to develop shared community involvement and in empowering young people. The mobile resource was particularly successful and has been incorporated as an element of the On Track project, now funded by the Children and Young People's Unit, which is operating in the Haverhill area. In response to the transport problems highlighted here, SACRE is also piloting a Moped Loan Scheme for young people.

The report contains valuable lessons for developers and project managers, as well as for practitioners. The main report and the addendum on criminality and anti-social behaviour in rural areas also offer a particular perspective on some aspects of rural crime and disorder and on the factors which affect perceptions and experiences of crime in rural areas.

The addendum report on criminality and anti-social behaviour in rural areas was not written for publication but is included here with the permission of the authors as it offers illuminating insight into aspects of crime as perceived, relatively unsystematically, in a small cluster of rural areas. As such, it does not set out to be definitive or generalisable.

Christine Lehman
Research, Development and Statistics Directorate

Acknowledgements

We would like to express our appreciation to the many people whose co-operation was essential in conducting this evaluation. Our thanks go to all those who agreed to be interviewed and gave so generously of their time. In addition we would like to thank the project staff who also answered our many queries with great patience and skill.

Dr E Doy
Di Gilbert
Dr L Maitland

Abbreviations

AG	Advisory Group
APW	Assistant Project Worker
Com Ed	Community Education
LAPs	Local Action Plans
SACRE	Suffolk Action for Communities in Rural England
SPW	Senior Project Worker
SCC	Suffolk County Council

Contents

Introduction

The *'Empowering Young People in Rural Suffolk'* project, one of a group of local initiatives funded by the Home Office Programme Development Unit, targeted young people aged 13 to 20 living in rural Suffolk and aimed to improve access to local services, increase involvement in civic life and decision-making, and reduce anti-social behaviour. The project initially covered three areas (called patches). Patch One was to run for two years, Patches Two and Three for three years. During the first year of the project there were innumerable personnel difficulties in Patch Three resulting in both project workers leaving, one due to ill-health. It was decided that this patch should be dropped from the project because it was felt that it would be too difficult to find replacement personnel. The funding from this patch was transferred to Patch One, enabling it to run for three years and thus finish at the same time as Patch Two.

The evaluation methods

The evaluation methodology was qualitative, incorporating semi-structured interviews, case studies and non-participant observation. Over the three years of the project a total of 64 interviews were conducted with 94 respondents, of whom 41 were adults and 53 young people. Six case studies of young people were also undertaken. Twelve interventions were observed.

Background and project content

Concerns had been raised by rural youth workers with Suffolk Action for Communities in Rural England (SACRE), and Community Education about the lack of facilities for young people; feelings of powerlessness by young people; their lack of a 'voice' in their communities; increasing vandalism and deteriorating relationships between young people and adults in the community. There were concerns that young people were experiencing lack of self-esteem which could create situations in which they became vulnerable to substance misuse or succumbed to criminal behaviour.

The rural patches that were selected as project sites were chosen primarily because SACRE already had a sound grasp of local difficulties in these geographical areas.

Young people interviewed were knowledgeable about the role of parish councils and many knew councillors by name. Yet they were disillusioned by the system, believing that parish councillors did not care and tended only to cater for older people. Feelings ranged from anger to apathy.

Interview data showed that in some villages there was a breakdown in communication between young people and adults in the community. Some adults were abusive towards young people; some, notably older village residents, felt intimidated by young people, particularly those in groups. Young people's attitudes towards older residents were also worrying. Youth crime was low in the patches, but incidents of anti-social behaviour gave rise to a heightened perception of crime, a particular fear for older people.

Lack of public transport was seen to be a major barrier to young people accessing facilities.

Project aims

The aims of the project were to:

- improve access to services targeted at young people in rural areas

- promote the involvement of young people in civic life and local decision-making in rural areas

- reduce criminality and crime in rural Suffolk.

The overall objective of the project was:

- to establish a community where young people have a sense of 'ownership' and self worth in which criminality does not have an opportunity to take hold.

Under the theme of citizenship, it was hoped that young people would form youth fora such as Youth Parish Councils/Youth Neighbourhood Watch and that some initiatives would bring young people and older residents together, thus promoting community integration.

Project management

Despite high levels of interest and goodwill, there were problems in translating ideas into workable practice. A management hiatus from the onset of the project, coupled with a less than committed Advisory Group and intransigent personnel problems had an effect on the project.

Youth workers, as opposed to community development officers, were employed as project workers.

The project co-ordinator role was combined with that of senior project worker (SPW) on one patch.

There was a persistent lack of understanding about the aims of the project.

The two patches were set up differently: one had a mobile provision which called at villages and acted like a magnet to young people. On the other patch, the project workers had no base from which to work and no meeting place protected from the weather.

The interventions

The project engaged with approximately 200 young people over three years and most of the young people interviewed felt they had been empowered, although there were one or two exceptions.

Citizenship has been achieved in several areas where young people are working for the benefit of others and/or fundraising for the wider community.

One formally constituted Youth Forum has been formed. Three youth clubs have youth representation on their management committees. Post project, one Youth Village Hall Committee has been formed.

The mobile provision was extremely successful at engaging with young people. The patch that operated without this facility struggled to engage with them.

Pubs emerged as a youth facility with the support of both publicans and parents alike and played a positive role in the community in the absence of other youth provision.

These achievements were realised in spite of serious implementation problems. Early in the project's life, a decision-making vacuum opened up, created by a lack of Advisory Group guidance. This vacuum was filled by decisions about interventions from the project workers. This resulted in the project becoming 'bottom up' and therefore reactive, not proactive.

Rather than young people being referred to the project, project workers had to literally 'find' young people to volunteer to take part in the interventions.

There was an over ambitious range of interventions over a too widespread geographical area, without the necessary time to implement them and a lack of coherent strategy. This led to several interventions having to be dropped from the project.

Conclusions

The project should be replicated in other rural areas but taking into account the lessons which can be learned from this project:

- From the outset of a project it is crucial to develop clear written plans and guidelines with key stages built in for review and 'hands on' line management which is proactive.

- If community development is a project aim, community development workers need to be employed.

- The co-ordinator/SPW role should not be combined.

- Considerable thought should be given to the project areas. If crime reduction is an aim, it would be better to focus on areas where this is an issue.

- If the volunteer approach is taken – that is, there are no referrals to a project, – it is unlikely that the 'harder edged' youth are going to take part; – the only failure the mobile had was with a group such as this.

- Adherence to one model – be it 'bottom up' or 'top down' – is limiting, a combination of both may be a preferable approach.

- The way the patches are set up is crucial. This project was almost two different projects; certainly this is how it felt to the project workers. One patch had the advantages of the mobile and the co-ordinator as a senior project worker. The other project workers had no base, with no venues undercover to meet new contacts in some villages.

- Rural community projects need to engage with local adult decision- makers because they are such an integral part of village life. Rural youth empowerment needs their support. The successful youth fora have come about in villages where councils were receptive to the idea. Parish councils, whilst important, are not the only local decision-makers. If they show no interest others should be sought out, such as community councils and village hall committees.

- There is a need for affordable, regular rural bus services which also offer some late night services to enable young people to use evening facilities in the closest towns. The comments from our interviewees endorse that view. Poor public transport is an issue which affects the whole population, not just young people and, whilst rural car ownership is high, the groups with the least access to cars are elderly and young people. The view was expressed that rural public transport should be seen, in part, as a social service.

The case studies

Six case studies of young people are provided which give a flavour of the impact of the project.

1   Methodology

Introduction

The format of this report is as follows: after the methodology section, the project is set in its location and context. This is followed by a section which evaluates the management aspect of the project, examining the role of the managing agency, the Advisory Group (hereafter referred to as AG) and the Programme Development Unit (PDU). An evaluation of the service delivery aspect of the project – the activities termed interventions – is then presented year by year. Finally, project outcomes are analysed, with a concluding section which looks at the lessons to be learned from this project should it be replicated.

The project initially covered three areas (called patches). Patch One was to run for two years, Patches Two and Three for three years. During the first year of the project there were many personnel difficulties in Patch Three resulting in both project workers leaving. It was decided to drop this patch from the project because it was felt that it would be too difficult to find replacement personnel. The funding from this patch was transferred to Patch One, enabling it to run for three years and thus finish at the same time as Patch Two. Because very little took place in Patch Three prior to its removal from the project, the evaluation, and therefore this report, covers Patches One and Two.

The evaluation structure and methods

This was a developmental project and process evaluation was important. The 'why' and 'how' of project development was the focus, that is 'what happened to whom, where, when, and why, and (if applicable) why not'. The evaluation methodology was therefore qualitative, incorporating semi-structured interviews, case studies and non-participant observation. At the beginning of the project, semi-structured interviews took place with AG members and 'key' people in other agencies. During the period of the project, the evaluators attended AG meetings and provided summaries of evaluation progress. The evaluators also attended an away day for project staff and used the method of non-participant observation at selected project interventions such as mobile visits (see Appendix A for a description of the mobile), council meetings and summer sessions. A Parish Council workshop was also attended.

Semi-structured interviews with groups of young people were arranged at the beginning of the project to ascertain the existing problems, and at the end, focusing on the intended and unintended outcomes of the project. The original plan was that each group would be composed of ten young people. In the event, the groups were smaller as it proved to be too difficult to arrange in such a large, sparsely populated geographical area. Over the lifetime of the project it was not possible to interview identical groups because some of the young people had left the project as they became older, but most of those interviewed at the beginning were also interviewed at the end. In addition, six in-depth retrospective case studies were carried out with selected young people.

Semi-structured group interviews were additionally carried out with parish councillors, business representatives and other adult members of the community; there were repeat interviews with the latter. The project workers were interviewed at the beginning of the project, half-way through, and at the end. Extra meetings were held with the project workers during the project so that the evaluators could clarify issues arising during the period. Statistics were collated as background information and a database was constructed in order to track interventions.

A report was submitted to the PDU at the end of the first year and *Emerging Findings* was submitted mid-term in order to assist stakeholders in obtaining further funding at the end of the project.

Although there was some feedback to the project, the evaluation was not deliberately formative and did not feed substantially into the development process. This was at times frustrating. The evaluators were appointed after the commencement of the project and it would have been preferable if the evaluators had been in place at the beginning. The project workers commented that they also would have preferred the evaluators to be more formative, especially (as this report shows) as the management of the project was weak. However, this level of involvement by the evaluators might have resulted in other problems.

Over the three years of the project a total of 64 interviews were conducted with 94 respondents, of whom 41 were adults and 53 were young people. Six case studies of young people were also undertaken. Twelve interventions were observed.

Project location and aim

Funding was made available by the Home Office Programme Development Unit in 1996 for innovative local projects relating to early intervention to prevent and reduce criminality. 'Empowering Young People' was one of six projects selected for three-year funding. The project was based in rural Suffolk and targeted young people aged 13 to 20 years of age. Concerns had been raised by rural youth workers with Suffolk Action for Communities in Rural England (hereafter referred to as SACRE) and Community Education (ComEd) about the lack of facilities for young people; feelings of powerlessness by young people; their lack of a 'voice' in their communities; increasing vandalism and deteriorating relationships between young people and adults in the community. There were concerns that young people were experiencing lack of self-esteem which could create situations in which they became vulnerable to substance misuse or succumb to criminal behaviour. In other words, young people were feeling community/social exclusion and there was the fear that young people might react to this exclusion with anti-social/criminal behaviour. The rural patches which were selected as project sites were chosen primarily because SACRE already had a sound grasp of local difficulties in these geographical areas.

The original aims of the project were to:

- improve access to services targeted at young people in rural areas

- promote the involvement of young people in civic life and local decision -making in rural areas

- reduce criminality and crime in rural Suffolk.

The overall objective of the project was:

> to establish a community where young people have a sense of 'ownership' and self worth in which criminality does not have an opportunity to take hold.

However, it soon became clear that there was little by way of *criminal* behaviour in the areas in which the project worked, but there was some *anti-social* behaviour, usually when young people congregated at the bus stop or shop doorway. This behaviour was frightening to older residents, increasing their perceptions of crime. The third aim of the project was therefore amended to: *reduce anti-social behaviour.*

The project was funded from four sources: the Home Office Programme Development Unit provided £98,324; the Rural District Council and Lloyds TSB each provided half of the £36,500 funding for the mobile provision for one patch and ComEd provided 'in kind' support valued at £20,000. The main focus of interest for the PDU was "...the extent of involvement by both young people and adults achieved by the project; the effectiveness of youth forums and councils; the effectiveness of the mobile youth provision and of peer education and the extent of usefulness of inter-agency work" (PDU/evaluator correspondence 18/11/96).

Project structure and method

Each of the three areas was staffed by one senior project worker (SPW) and one assistant project worker (APW). These posts were part-time for 40 weeks per year. A project co-ordinator was also appointed and this post was coupled with the SPW post in one of the patches. The co-ordinator post was also part time and became full time in January, 1998. All the appointees were experienced youth workers with the exception of the co-ordinator who was new to both youth work and project management. The majority of the project workers also worked for ComEd as youth workers in their primary employment. The project also afforded the opportunity for new inter-agency working practices to be explored.

Rather than young people being referred to this project, they had, quite literally, to be found. Project staff aimed to do this through detached youth work and by visiting local schools and youth clubs. Patch Two also had the benefit of the mobile provision. Once contact was made with interested young people the project aimed to work with them on peer group initiatives to build self-esteem and tackle issues such as criminality and substance misuse, involve them in local civic structures where appropriate and provide advice on a range of issues from health to careers. The project was 'sold' to the young people as an opportunity to give them a voice in their community. It was hoped that ultimately young people would form youth fora such as Youth Parish Councils/Youth Neighbourhood Watch and that some initiatives would bring young people and older residents together, thus promoting community integration.

Background and project context

Appendix B contains further background information on the patches; Appendices C, D and E contain the tables to which the figures below refer.

Village profiles

Population statistics show that between the 1991 Census and figures updated in 1997 from Suffolk County Council, the population in the 13 villages covered by the project has remained virtually unchanged: 10,020 (1991) and 10,190 (1997). The stability of the population is evidenced by the fact that there was an increase in Suffolk's population of only 5.3 per cent between 1981 and 1991 (Census County Report: Suffolk (Part 1) OPCS [1991] London HMSO). In the 1991 Census, as a proportion of adults, young people were: 5-15 13per cent; 16-17 2.8 per cent; 18-29 16.7 per cent.

Of the total dwelling stock, the majority, 65 per cent were owner occupied; 13 per cent were privately rented, including from Housing Associations; 12.5 per cent in use as Local Authority housing. In six of the 13 villages, there is a small number of dwellings not used as a main residence, 3.25 per cent.

The villages also show a high level of economic activity and a low level of unemployment and people on government schemes. For example, of the total males and females aged over 16 and economically active (4,769), 67 per cent of males and 48 per cent of females are in full-time employment; 2.9 per cent of males and 38 per cent of females are in part-time work; 21.5 per cent of males and 9 per cent of females are self-employed.

Crime

Crime figures are difficult to assess because of different methods of gathering data. Local constabularies collect data on a different geographical basis to data from national crime statistics. Although Suffolk Constabulary do not include details such as age of the offender in with the offence, some offences are particularly associated with young people. Criminal damage is one, and taking that as an example, for the villages in question, all criminal damage incidents for 1997 are less than a third of the rate of England and Wales (see Appendix F for a breakdown of the figures). As this is an offence closely associated with young people, the low figures are indicative of the low youth crime rate on the patches. The figures given also include adult offenders, so it is feasible that these offences were not committed by young people in the age range of the project.

Young Peoples' Perceptions

As stated previously, the impetus for the original bid to the PDU was the concern about young people's lack of (in sociological terms) activity spaces, their lack of 'voice' in their community and deteriorating relationships with village adults. The first round of evaluator interviews with young people showed that this concern was well founded. It was also clear from these interviews that young people held very negative views of parish councillors, and that lack of public transport was a major problem. What follows are some of the findings from those interviews.

The village pub as a youth facility

In four villages the pub was the focal point for young people. However, this was not the cause for concern it might appear to be initially. It was not a case of young people involved in under-age drinking sessions or 'down the pub' when parents believed them to be elsewhere. It was the case that in these villages the pub is the legitimate, local provision. Young people are using the pub as their meeting place and recreation facility, for pool, snooker, cards and the like, with parental and publican approval. Parents approved because they knew their offspring were not being served alcohol and, as one parent put it, "at least when they are in the local pub you know they are staying in the village". Another commented that, unlike other young people he knew of, young people in their village were "not 'touring' pubs and having alcohol bought for them".

It was also the case that the publicans were very involved with the young people in a community sense and with their activities, for example in putting on discos at the weekend or helping with fund-raising activities. One publican felt that letting young people use the pub was 'educational' in that it encouraged a more responsible, 'continental attitude' towards drinking, and young people would not 'go mad' when they reached the legal age of consent for drinking. She felt that the Children's Certificate had a role to play here and that the dual use of venues such as pubs should be made easier where there is no other village provision.

Young people's attitude towards parish councils

Young people had considerable knowledge about local politics. For example, children as young as ten years old knew what the role of the parish council was in terms of service provision. Many of them knew parish councillors by name; some knew them on a personal level as 'my friend's aunty' and some were related to parish councillors. Given that these are rural villages with the personal proximities that entails, this is not perhaps surprising. That these young people are so 'clued up' about the local democratic process is in itself quite a positive thing. However, they were already disillusioned with the system:

They don't listen to kids.

The parish council call the shots.

The parish council focuses on the needs of old people.

The parish council is a bunch of old people.

Feelings ranging from anger to apathy were apparent. The majority felt that their parish council did not recognise nor care about young people's needs, that they did not listen to young people, that they were more concerned with elderly people, and that parish councillors were themselves in that category.

There is some evidence from the study to explain why young people hold these negative feelings towards parish councils. Obstructions to the setting up of youth clubs, refusals to let young people use, for example, village pavilions, difficulties with using recreation grounds and/or football pitches were issues that the young people had to contend with. Of course, parish councils had reasons for these 'obstructions' – the football pitch was league standard, not for kicking a ball about on, the oak tree on the green needed to be preserved, insurance problems with the use of certain buildings were some of the reasons given. However, these explanations were often not given to the young people.

Young people's attitudes towards older residents

Young people's attitudes towards their parish council/councillors were in general a reflection of their attitudes to older residents. Young people felt under suspicion:

People walk their dogs to keep an eye on us

If we go to 'the rec' we are moaned at so we just 'hang around' in the street getting wet and cold.

If we do anything in the village old people whinge at us.

Old people approach us with...their dogs and zimmer frames...

Old people blame us for litter, vandalism and noise.

This village feels like a retirement home.

Young people gave examples of riding their mopeds on a dirt track and a car park and older residents coming out and videoing them, and their (few) discos having to finish early to placate older residents.

Transport

Lack of public transport was an issue raised by all groups of interviewees (and repeated more than once by some). Little or no public transport was felt to be a main barrier to accessing facilities for young people in nearby centres, which caused boredom, which in turn can lead to anti-social behaviour. In one of the villages there were no problems for or with young people apart from the lack of public transport which made them even more isolated. The alternative for them was to rely on lifts by their parents, or for the older young people, their friends. Although some facilities were 'only a bike ride' away, it was felt that it was no longer safe to cycle due to the volume and speed of cars on rural roads.

Although they have small populations, some villages are very spread out, and a bus stop can be a mile away from parts of the village. This, coupled with a sparse, irregular and sometimes unreliable service, added to the difficulties. Recently transport had improved in some villages but at the expense of others where the service had declined.

It is against this background that the project was set.

3   Project management

If support and goodwill for the project were any criteria, SACRE had these in abundance. Enthusiasm for the project and a desire to see it succeed by the management of SACRE was evident from the outset and they drew support from a range of key agencies who had high expectations for the outcome.

Several members of the key agencies hoped the project would provide them with examples of good practice which could be replicated throughout the county and the country. It was further hoped that the successes of the project would influence local and national government policies. If any interventions did not succeed, lessons could be learned. The main hope was that the project would have a long lasting and beneficial effect on young people with foundations for other projects. There was optimism that, if there were barriers, these could be overcome.

These expectations generate their own kind of pressure. Such high expectations often fail to take into account the complexity of translating 'good ideas' into workable practices. In the process of developing a project, there will inevitably be successes and failures. Personnel and personalities can hinder or help. Interventions which seemed worthwhile and 'doable' turn out to be impossible. There were further pressures in that SACRE was entering territory in which it had little experience – a project which was working with young people. However, this potential weakness was offset by inviting onto the AG members who had professional expertise.

SACRE Management

The onset of a project is the time when senior management involvement is the most crucial to its success. It is a time when the best laid plans can become unstuck without strong leadership to set realistic objectives and priorities. It was unfortunate that the commencement of this project was marred by the lack of continuity of line management within SACRE at executive level. This, coupled with the appointment of a co-ordinator with little project management experience, had a significant impact on the way in which the project developed, with implications down the line. It also made it difficult for the co-ordinator and the project workers to be effective at an early stage.

Early in the first year SACRE's Head of Development and Chair of the AG took sabbatical leave which left the new co-ordinator with four line managers in six months, one being the Chief Executive of SACRE who already had a heavy workload. The co-ordinator also had an additional difficulty of line management by ComEd in her role as project worker, and SACRE in her role as co-ordinator. During the second year, the Head of Development left and, after several months the new Chief Executive took the project to fruition. Of course these management changes could not have been foreseen at the Bid stage.

In addition, seemingly intransigent personnel problems with Patch Three (referred to in the Introduction) remained unresolved for several months and took up a disproportionate amount of management and AG time, which consequently led to delay in implementation.

The lack of continuity of management at the start-up period, together with the need for new project staff to be integrated, and valuable project time spent on personnel problems, led to a degree of drift at the outset of the project which had repercussions throughout its life.

The Advisory Group

Agencies represented on the Advisory Group (AG) are listed at Appendix G.

There was a potentially strong AG and a high degree of goodwill towards the project at the outset with a broad spectrum of agency representation from organisations throughout Suffolk.

In November 1996, the PDU summarised their view of the role of the AG thus: it would oversee the production and implementation of action plans; ensure partnerships; have budgetary oversight and be concerned with project continuance if successful. This was to change as there was much discussion as to what its responsibilities were to be and whether it should be called a steering group. At the third AG (April 1997) it was agreed that it would be a steering group (although still called an AG); it was not to be a 'working group' and members were not expected to take on areas of work but could opt to do so if they wished.

It became apparent that many of the agency representatives had been unaware of the bid and, once they were, they did not fully agree with its aims. This factor, combined with lack of 'hands on' management at the beginning of the project may account, to some extent, for the unstructured development of a large number of interventions spread across widely spaced geographical regions with an unrealistic time allocation for their completion. It may also account for the AG failing to take 'ownership' of the project. This issue is expanded on later in the report.

This lack of continuity of management in SACRE was also reflected within the AG itself. A significant problem for the project was the number of changes over time to the composition of the AG, together with a falling off in attendance. Representatives from each agency were rarely the same at each meeting, in part due to internal changes, which led to the need to re-cap in meetings on what had taken place earlier. Attendance declined. Most of the original group either no longer attended or sent representatives. To try to encourage greater participation by the AG, an 'away day' was held. Unfortunately no AG member turned up. Because of this, it was decided not to involve the majority of the members any further and it was officially agreed to reduce the AG to a core group with the inclusion of the project workers.

AG lack of 'ownership' of the project may be partly due to a degree of disillusionment which set in with both the nature of the project and the progress being made, and partly to a growing confusion about roles, aims and objectives. Interviews with AG members in 1997 produced mixed views about its role and its effectiveness. Some members felt it was to act in an advisory capacity and to offer expertise when called for. Others thought its role should be more proactive, steering the project to ensure the aims and objectives were met. Some did not fully understand its role, nor their own role on it, and felt marginal to the project.

There were a number of different views on the aims and objectives of the project, for example whether it was to be crime prevention, empowerment, structural integration, citizenship or effective practice. Only three of the members' answers referred to the aims as stated in the bid. In addition, some members were not clear what the overall perspective of the project was, with most answers sharing a common feature of being abstract, for example, 'dissolving prejudices' 'taking young people forward' and so on. Only two members of the AG thought that the interventions would bring about the aims of the project, with some elements being more successful than others. The themes of innovation and structural integration became the subject of debate early on in the project and led to a degree of confusion. The project was viewed as 'innovative for Suffolk'. The term 'structural integration' tended to fade away as the project progressed, to be replaced by 'citizenship'. Other concerns raised were whether the project could be completed in time given the geographic spread of the interventions, and the number of goals to be met. However, one of the AG members, who became the Chair after the SACRE Head of Development left and remained Chair until he left his agency, was consistently and strongly supportive of the co-ordinator and the project workers.

Action Plans based on the bid had been requested at the initial meeting in November 1996. Developing these Action Plans took up a considerable amount of the co-ordinator's time and they were only agreed in principle in June 1997 with amendments requested.

Having developed the Action Plans, keeping track of the various interventions within them proved to be difficult. The AG asked repeatedly for a system of cross-referencing from the quarterly progress reports to the agreed plan. There was, however, some room for flexibility because it was a development project. Part of the problem was that although quarterly reports were submitted and referred to various interventions, there was no consistency. From the point of view of the AG and the management of the project, this made it very difficult to comprehend what progress the project was making, which interventions were continuing and which had been dropped. Some interventions appeared, later to 'disappear' with no explanation, unless picked up by a member of the AG. Senior and middle management appeared unable to grasp the importance of consistency and this was not achieved until January 1998, when the interventions were related to the database.

The Role of the PDU

There was some confusion about the role of the PDU among both AG members and project workers. For AG members, this may have been because of the lack of continuity within the AG referred to above. Some did not understand whether the PDU were AG members or passive facilitators. Since the PDU sometimes chaired meetings and sometimes did not, some were confused as to whether they were part of the management team. One project worker felt they should have had much more of a 'hands on' approach.

4.   The interventions

Appendix H provides a full list of planned interventions and their outcomes in table format.

Year One: Setting up the interventions

Over the first few months of the project the co-ordinator, working in conjunction with the project workers and with guidance from the AG, was required to draw up Local Action Plans (LAPs). These were in effect the mechanism through which the project aims were to be met. Project worker input was considered vital because most of them were experienced youth workers and had local knowledge. The LAPs were to form the main activities of the project – the service delivery aspect. This was a pivotal stage, but it proved to be difficult and a decision-making vacuum opened up. This vacuum, created by lack of AG guidance, was filled by the project workers and, while they were all excellent face-to-face youth workers, they were not planners. This led to rather ambitious interventions being proposed, some of which did not match up to the aims of the project. This is not surprising because, at this stage, it appears that none of the project workers was aware of the project aims, as they had not seen the bid. The co-ordinator was aware of the aims but, because she was new to both youth work and management, she was badly in need of AG support at this juncture. The co-ordinator felt that, as fundholders, the PDU should have been a little more directive at this point and much clearer about what they wanted to see in the LAPs. The PDU, however, were reluctant to exercise too much influence over local plans which needed to be based on local knowledge and professional experience. The LAPs were returned to the project workers several times for amendment. All this had specific implications for the project:

- First, it caused frustration for the project workers and the co-ordinator because they could not see what was wrong with the LAPs. This was instrumental in bringing about a 'them and us' mentality from the project workers and co-ordinator towards the AG as a group (not necessarily as individuals). This perception improved slightly as the project progressed but hung over the relationship between AG and project workers for the life of the project.

- Second, because they were unaware of the wider aims of the project and knowing that its title was Empowering Young People in Rural Suffolk, the project workers took the empowerment of young people to be the project's *raison d'etre*.

To square with their youth worker philosophy they adopted a 'bottom up' as opposed to a 'top down' model as their working practice. It became almost a mantra that, to be empowered, young people could not be 'done to' and (under the theme 'giving young people a voice') ideas had to come from the young people themselves, with the project workers acting as facilitators. This, in turn, resulted in the project becoming reactive rather than proactive.

- Third, because the project workers were unaware of the community development aspect of the project, they did not propose interventions designed to bring young people and older adults together. Such interventions were discussed at an AG meeting and subsequently proposed by the PDU in a letter to the co-ordinator but she took these to be suggestions only and did not pursue them. Consequently this type of community integration was lost to the project, which focused on young people, although adults (usually parents and/or local councillors) were involved in some interventions.

The LAP delays, coupled with the AG discussions on clarifying project aims and its own remit, meant the project got off to a very slow start.

The main venue for village events was the village hall or recreation ground. Generally these two venues were under the auspices of the parish council, which meant that parish councils were going to have an important role in the project. So a two-pronged approach was planned. The project workers' sensible starting point was the place where young people are to be found in numbers – the local schools. Here they 'advertised' the project wares. In addition, all the parish councils in the patches were invited to a seminar where the project was to be explained and parish councils invited to take part. The seminar did not take place. Of the 41 councils invited, only six replied. The co-ordinator had planned a comprehensive seminar with speakers and workshops. Owing to the poor response, she cancelled the event. In some ways this was unfortunate because, from that point on, the project workers felt that the parish councils were not interested in the project, which was demoralising, and the early involvement of this important group was lost to the project. It may have been better to have continued with a scaled down seminar for the six interested councils because there would then have been the possibility of a 'snowball effect' – one council seeing what was happening in another village and becoming interested.

Finding young people met with mixed success. Patch Two had only one school to focus on because its catchment area was so large. The workers here also did more than visit the school; they conducted a survey at the school to ascertain young people's needs. The findings of the survey had an important impact on the project, as it became clear that young people did not want to be taken to facilities in a minibus, but would rather have a facility brought to their village. Hence the decision was made for this patch to buy and equip the mobile rather than purchase a minibus. All subsequent interventions on this patch stemmed from the on-going school visits. Once the mobile was operational, the workers had the benefit of parking it in the school grounds and inviting young people on board. This proved very attractive to young people. In the final part of Year One, the project workers spent time contacting young people throughout the patch via the mobile, listening to young people's ideas and in one or two villages firming up these ideas into plans. In two villages this involved helping young people set up a youth club, with youth representation on the management committee, and in another village it involved contributing to existing plans for a European youth event. Young people were also involved in drug awareness raising sessions.

Patch One had more difficulty in finding young people. It had to visit more schools and 'advertise' to smaller numbers over a wider area. It did not have the mobile as a 'travelling billboard' (as one project worker described it). Very few sustainable contacts came from these school visits, although the workers did have a few sessions with young people at one particular school. This patch continued to try to find young people through outreach work, street sessions and visiting existing youth clubs. In one village the project workers attended an existing youth club and spent several sessions there, having discovered a disaffected group of young people who wanted to provide a 'drop in' for other younger people to prevent them from becoming as disillusioned as they were. The SPW was optimistic at this point that the project could help this group become a youth forum. Contact had also been made with small numbers in some scattered villages and again the SPW was optimistic that in three villages there were young people interested in forming a patch youth forum. The project workers in this patch had also helped some young people negotiate a meeting place because their village hall had burned down.

The SPW also took part in two 'residentials'. These were successful multi-agency interventions in conjunction with ComEd and a voluntary youth organisation, Art 604. The local parish council endorsed the events and publicised them via parish newsletters and magazines. One, a weekend event, attracted 29 young people from six villages with an age range of 12 to 19 years. This intervention came about because young people expressed concerns at the lack of facilities for their age group. The residential was thus activity based, offering canoeing, rafting, underwater photography and the like. It was also felt that the setting would enable young people to build relationships with others from rural and urban areas. The second residential had 21 attenders from across the patch. This was not activity based, its focus being a youth perspective on village issues, transport, village integration and so forth. However, whilst extremely successful as 'one-off' interventions, there was no project follow up to these, although, of course, the other agencies involved may have continued to work with these young people.

But much of the outreach work and street sessions were proving unsuccessful in engaging young people in the project; in some cases no young people at all turned up.

Summary

The first year can be summed up as a slow start, followed by sustainable contact with some young people leading to successful interventions which met some aims of the project. Young people had been empowered in forming youth clubs, which had also involved them in citizenship via the contact they had with their local council. The mobile itself was a facility and so by definition it had met the aim of increasing youth access to facilities, while in the other patch the SPW had some potential youth fora members in mind and had made one-off contact with a considerable number of young people and publicised the project to some extent.

But problems were also in evidence. Parish councillors were not showing interest in the project, take up in one patch was low, project workers were feeling demoralised by the lack of AG involvement and one patch had been dropped from the project altogether.

Year Two: Progress of the interventions

This year saw the project move some interventions forward and withdraw from other successfully completed interventions. In Patch Two one youth club flourished during this year with very little further project involvement, and the young people here also became fundraisers for village-wide projects. The other youth club required continuing assistance from the project due to a steep dropout rate because the young people felt the youth club was not offering anything age appropriate. The project workers were able to engage with these young people by providing the mobile as a regular meeting place whilst acting as facilitators between the young people and the local council about the young people's idea for a BMX track.

The European event was successfully accomplished. This intervention was in partnership with ComEd and seven young people attended a community safety residential conference for young people in Belgium. It was part of a 20-year series of events involving European villages whose names are derivatives of Hearts of Oak. It was this village's first involvement. Young people were thus representing their village and their country. This intervention brought the whole community together in fund-raising events to send the young people to the residential and entailed the young people videoing village life for a presentation in Belgium. The fund raising was very successful and the young people donated a surplus amount to the local school. On their return the project workers helped the young people with a formal presentation of their experience to a public parish council meeting. The project also retained involvement in two other ways. First, the young people wanted to have a return event and project workers helped them formulate their ideas and second, two of the young people attended a youth worker training course put on by the project workers.

Contacts continued to be made across the patch and the idea of a youth forum was discussed with a particular group of very disaffected young people. In the event this did not materialise due to lack of continuity of involvement by these young people. This was the only intervention involving the mobile which struggled to attract or retain the interest of young people. Historically this village was different to others in the patches, as it had been a large military base. The population of young people was much higher and more cosmopolitan, it had higher criminality rates and a core of very disaffected youths. Whilst the project did attempt to engage them over quite a prolonged period, the lack of continuity of interest by young people made it almost impossible to do any sustainable work with this group. Project workers eventually switched to working at the existing youth club and assisted three young people to become members of the youth club committee. Young people were also given a two-page spread in the local magazine, so they achieved a voice in this way.

The mobile made several trips to a very remote village and facilitated discussions between young people and their parish council over a planned inter-village football competition. However, this did not materialise due to peer group disagreements and the project workers withdrew as they felt the young people here were beginning to rely on them too much. Following feedback from the evaluators, agreed by the AG, initial contact was made with perhaps the most disaffected group of young people the project was to engage with and the project workers started the time-consuming task of gaining their trust.

Patch One continued to have problems with take-up. A 'road show' was planned which entailed targeting villages with low take-up and several activities were arranged to encourage young people to engage with the project. This was not very successful, due mainly to lack of publicity and choice of venues. It appears, for example, that when the 'road show' went to the pub car park the young people were on the recreation ground and vice versa. However, some new contacts were made and where the project workers had a 'resident audience' – the school and youth club sessions – they were able to move interventions forward.

Drug awareness raising programmes were introduced, both at the youth clubs and the school sessions, and a quite comprehensive drugs misuse survey was undertaken by the APW. This was at the request of the county Substance Misuse Group (a multi- agency committee) which wanted a rural element to a wider survey. Findings from this were found to be in line with national trends. At one town school there was a youth council in operation and the project successfully facilitated the development of a rural arm to this council. The SPW also met young people and adults involved in a Youth Parish Council in a nearby town to discuss their experience of turning the idea into reality, which had taken two years.

The young people at the youth clubs mentioned above needed help to open up discussions with their parish councils with ideas on how to give young people a voice in their community, and in the early part of Year Two the project continued to take a facilitating role here. However, as the year progressed the project on this patch did not. The reasons why are discussed below.

It had become clear at the end of the first year that there were problems in Patch One and these became acute during Year Two. The SPW was under considerable pressure from his other employment as a youth worker. Some weeks he was committed to 56 hours in this job, which affected his commitment to the SACRE/PDU job. He was not putting in the hours and the problem was further compounded by some lack of delegation to the APW. Eventually, in Year Two she felt she had no choice but to make a formal complaint. The SPW went through the full disciplinary procedure of verbal warnings, written warnings and finally a disciplinary meeting. However, whilst the cause was theoretically being dealt with nothing appears to have been put in place to deal with the effects. Work on this patch entailed long journeys, sometimes in the evenings, to remote villages to meet young people in open spaces. The APW felt unable to continue with this sort of work alone for security reasons, management offered no solution to the problem, and therefore by the end of Year Two the project was petering out in this patch.

Summary

The second year saw one patch develop quite successfully in villages where it had made contact in the first year and begin to engage a very disaffected group of young people in another village, whilst the other patch continued to have problems which were not resolved.

Parish councils per se were still not involved in the project and the postponed parish council workshop did not materialise this year, the co-ordinator making the decision to target smaller numbers of councils for local workshops in the early part of Year Three instead.

Year Three: Intervention Outcomes

Early in this year the twice postponed parish workshop took place. Several parishes attended a round table discussion during which the project was outlined. Some success stories were given by two young people who addressed the meeting to explain how the project had helped them set up youth clubs in their villages. Some of the attending parishes were already involved in the project as these were the areas in which the youth clubs had been set up. Of the parishes not already involved, none followed up. It was perhaps a little late in the life of the project to try to bring new parishes on board.

The problems of commitment from one SPW continued during the third year and in this patch the project did no more than limp along for the best part of the final year. The SPW continued to have excellent ideas but they never developed beyond that. He also embarked on another unsuccessful 'road show' which failed to attract young people for precisely the same reasons as in Year Two. The APW was undertaking a DipHE in Youth Work and as part of it she was working with a group of young people on a volunteering project. It was decided by the AG that this work, 'the Rovin' Project', could be supported by the project.

The SPW and the co-ordinator left in the summer of Year Three. Neither were replaced at this late stage but both remaining project workers were promoted, one becoming co-ordinator and SPW for the remaining period, the other taking the title SPW for her patch. She continued to work on the Rovin' Project for the remainder of the final year. (It was named Rovin' Project because a team of young volunteers travelled to where they were needed.) This was a successful intervention in which young volunteers worked to provide something of benefit to others. One task involved three young women transforming a room in a communal building. They were involved with all aspects of the task from planning and costing through to carrying out the decorating. Other voluntary work was at the planning stage at the end of the project but will continue as this was an inter-agency intervention and the other agency will carry on the work with the young women. Case Study One provides some detail on the impact of the project.

All other interventions in this patch ceased, leaving the youth club contacts somewhat puzzled and disillusioned with the project, several young people commenting that the project had no impact whatsoever in their village. One expressed the view that the project was actually damaging as it promised but did not deliver and has merely reinforced the view that adults let young people down. It must be noted here that the view of the project worker is slightly different. She believes this intervention ceased because the young people stopped attending. Conflicting views are, of course, difficult to judge. We can only say that the perspective of the young people was given to us in separate interviews with young people who did not know each other. Case Study Two provides more detail of the view of one of the disillusioned young people.

Although some young people commented on the lack of project impact in their community, in one case there has been an interesting development. The project had a brief life in this particular community in Year One. However post project, that is two years later, the Village Hall Committee is setting up a Youth Village Hall Committee. The young people who were interviewed credited this solely to the project because, although it only raised the village profile of young people briefly, the 'youth voice' seeds were sown and have now come to fruition. It is worth noting that the parish council in this village declined to take part in the project on the basis that it had no young people (parish council/evaluator correspondence 9/12/97). Village Hall Committee members, on the other hand, knew some young people in the village and were receptive to the idea of youth fora.

The other patch focused on two villages during the final year and carried the interventions forward to very successful outcomes. It continued to support the young people with their BMX plans. These had not come to fruition by the time the project ceased, due to the fact that the land which they needed was a preservation area, but the village profile of young people had been raised to such an extent that the parish council consulted them over a Lottery bid for further facilities and young people were invited to formally present their ideas formally to the parish council on other matters.

In the second village the project had its biggest success. Over the year the project facilitated meetings between young people and adults in the community and young people and their parish council, the outcome being a formally constituted youth forum. In conjunction with adults, members of this disaffected group of young people, some of whom were threatening older residents, are now co-executive members of the youth forum. They have successfully raised hundreds of pounds for a children's facility in the village and are currently negotiating to have a caravan as a 'drop in' for their own age group.

In sum, the final year saw some successful outcomes but also some disappointments.

Before moving on to the analysis of the outcomes, acknowledgment must be made of the personal esteem in which all the project workers were held by the young people. Many, in the final round of interviews, wanted to make the point that the attitude of the project staff was excellent and they clearly had the respect of the young people. Even where the outcomes were disappointing, at the level of face-to-face working, young people had nothing but praise for project staff. Several, including adults, also commented on the helpfulness of ComEd in the setting up of the youth clubs and several civic leaders expressed their appreciation at something as prestigious as the Home Office showing interest in their community. (One interviewee had two specific points she wished to be brought to the attention of the Home Office. These have been included as Appendix I.)

5.

Analysis of project outcomes

When looking at outcomes, it must be recognised just how much project time and energy had to go into simply making contact with young people, because there were no referrals and often no facilities to focus on. The amount of time it was going to take to find young people was seriously underestimated. Further, project workers had no way of knowing in advance if contacts, once made, would lead to sustained involvement by the young people or achieve project goals. In many cases these contacts did not. For example, sometimes when young people attended an intervention they turned out to be outside the target age group, or they were within the age group but simply did not want sustained involvement with the project, or there was no continuity of young people i.e. different young people turned up at each session, thus making it very difficult to follow up ideas. It must also be recognised that the project workers had to undertake a good deal of travel, as these were very large rural patches. However, despite considerable set backs, the project did achieve some notable outcomes, most of which met some or all of the project aims.

Extent of involvement by young people and adults

The project made 'contact' with several hundred young people if the two surveys are taken into account. However, a more meaningful figure is the number of young people who actually engaged with the project in a direct way; this was approximately 200. Adult numbers were approximately 20, mainly parents and local councillors involved by dint of the youth clubs set up (but of course many more were interviewed so had involvement in the project in this way). The adult group which never became involved with the project was older residents. As stated earlier, this element of community integration was not included in the LAPs, but was raised in a letter to the co-ordinator which she took to be a suggestion only: she did not act on it. The project workers themselves were unaware that this was ever intended and, as they pointed out in final evaluation interviews, this type of work requires different skills and is more the remit of a community development officer, not a youth worker. They would not have been comfortable with this aspect, one stating categorically that he would not have undertaken such work. This raises the issue of staff recruitment and the project worker referred to above felt that a considerable weakness of the project was 'faulty' recruitment practice. He was employed as a face-to-face youth worker but found that much of his time had to be spent on committees because the project needed to make links with other agencies for exit strategy purposes. He said that this was not made clear to him at the interview for the post. He was not at ease with this aspect of the work and it adversely affected his perspective of the project and his motivation. He viewed his incorporation onto the AG as an additional burden and believes that all the committee work prevented him from applying his youth worker skills and training. He felt the project tried to mould project workers into something they were not.

The effectiveness of youth fora and councils

If one takes youth fora in its widest sense and includes issue specific fora, the project has had successful outcomes in three villages. Two are youth club committees, which later promoted citizenship. One has a slightly wider remit and is seen by the young people as a youth forum, and is active in fund raising for village projects. In all three cases the project objective – *to establish a community where young people have a sense of 'ownership' and self worth in which criminality does not have an opportunity to take hold* – has been met. Interview data confirmed that the forming of these fora have meant a great deal to the young people concerned and Case Studies Three, Four and Five give a richer picture of their impact. In the case of the youth clubs, one had temporarily ceased by the end of the project due to lack of parental involvement and the other was having problems with drop out rates, but these problems are part and parcel of rural youth club life and interviewees, both adult and young people, felt that these difficulties would be overcome. As for the youth forum, it was set up towards the end of the life of the project and, at the time of writing, it was too early to be able to evaluate its long-term effectiveness. However, it has operated effectively to date. One initial problem that was overcome was a tendency for adults to try to 'take over' the joint committee. The project workers successfully acted as arbitrators between the young people and adults and this issue was resolved satisfactorily. Long term effectiveness depends on the sustainability of these interventions. The mechanisms are now in place and there have already been smooth personnel changes whereby younger young people have come on to the committee as older ones have moved on or moved away.

The effectiveness of the mobile youth provision

The mobile was extremely effective; indeed it is difficult to see how anything could have happened in the remote villages without the mobile provision. With one exception, wherever it went it acted like a magnet to young people who to a person in the evaluation interviews had nothing but praise for it. The following quotes are representative of the general view:

It was educational and fun.

Great, learned about the community, got careers information.

Made drug awareness raising posters, really good. Had information on lots of lots of issues.

The mobile itself was enough in our village – parents liked it as well.

The leaflets were useful.

The mobile was really good.

The mobile was great. Everybody liked it.

Case Study Six gives one young person's perspective on the mobile in more detail.

Although this report does not draw an evaluative comparison between the patches, it was clearly much more difficult for the patch without the mobile; this point is returned to later in the report.

Peer education

While peer education was originally one of the main planks of the project, in the event not a great deal of this took place in any organised way. At some interventions there were not many peers. However, the project workers pointed out that informal peer education through discussion of issues took place at many sessions. The most striking intervention where this did take place formally was where rural and urban young people were brought together for a role play session in which young people were 'confronted' with finding out that their sibling was taking drugs/involved in criminal acts such as shoplifting. The role play was also videoed, thus allowing the whole group to discuss their 'responses' to the situations with which they had been presented. In the final evaluation interviews with young people they had very positive comments about this session. Other drug awareness raising sessions involved an interactive computer package, and these sessions received similar positive comments. These interviews were two years after the events and the impact made by the sessions was clearly still with the interviewees.

Inter-agency working

Appendix J provides the names of other agencies connected with the project

Inter-agency working had mixed success. Project staff spent considerable time on multi-agency committees spreading the word about the project and this resulted in the forming of some new partnerships for SACRE which will remain beyond the life of the project. On the ground, some interventions successfully ran in conjunction with other agencies – the European intervention with ComEd and the Rovin' Project with 'Haverhill Making A Difference' for example. The police were very willing to take part in a planned youth/parish councillors day session. This was one of the interventions which never materialised, owing to the problems with one SPW, previously discussed. However, even after one postponement and eventual cancellation the police still indicated their willingness to take part had there been a rescheduled event.

Where there is disappointment felt by some interviewees, it is at the lack of inter-agency working at management level. The AG members did not act as ambassadors for the project and there is the view from some interviewees that some agencies represented on the AG were simply there to keep an eye on SACRE and may have wanted to see it fail. This has to be set in context. Initially, both SACRE and ComEd had bids in to the PDU for funding. As both could not succeed ComEd withdrew its bid and became a partner in the SACRE bid. As stated earlier, the project was also SACRE's first move into youth work and, as such, there was always the danger that it might be seen to be treading on the toes of agencies already working in that area. SACRE's intent was to complement ComEd's youth work, not usurp it. This partnership worked well at ground level, but at management level it was a more uneasy relationship. Some interviewees still hold the view that SACRE's interest in the project was merely a way for that organisation to expand its territory. Organisation theory suggests territory guarding based on power relations often simmers under the surface in agency relationships. In this respect this project was a text book case. The project may have reinforced existing power relations rather than facilitated a more co-operative way of working and hardened views generally as to the effectiveness of voluntary and statutory partnerships. Whilst projects in themselves may be new, they do not exist in isolation but take place within the context of existing agency relationships and their histories.

Exit Strategies

Exit strategies proved difficult. In part this relates to a misunderstanding. For quite some time, whenever exit strategies were discussed at AG meetings, it was in terms of the managing agency seeking further funding to carry on the project after the expiry of Home Office funding. Much of the Co-ordinator's time in the third year was spent on this. Exit strategies related to how the project might leave something sustainable behind when an intervention withdrew, were never really addressed. Some interventions were one-offs, some ended because project workers exited due to young people becoming 'too reliant', some petered out because of the problems with one SPW. Clearly exit strategies were not even an issue here. Where youth fora have been established the formally constituted committees are entities which will continue beyond the life of the project. In this respect there were exit strategies.

Conclusions

For the most part, the young people who engaged with the project have been empowered, and the more perceptive among them observed that the evaluation interviews themselves have given them a voice through this report. Citizenship has been successful in several areas where young people are now working with parish councils and have undertaken voluntary work for the benefit of others in the community. Community integration has been achieved to a degree. Youth fora have brought this about in some respects, but the youth-older adults element did not materialise. However, in one or two villages, young people have been left feeling disempowered rather than empowered.

There are several noteworthy achievements and the project should be replicated. At the same time there are lessons to be learned for the future.

- Evaluation of the management of the project shows a need to develop at a very early stage clear written plans and guidelines with key stages built in for review; 'hands on' line management which is pro-active; developed priorities; realistic and achievable timetables; strong leadership of the AG in order for it to fulfil its potential; 'ownership' of the project; the employment and development of appropriate personnel.

- If community development is a project aim, community development workers need to be employed. As one interviewee intimated, if youth workers are employed they carry out youth work. If what is wanted is community development between young people and older adults, project staff with skills in both areas need to be employed. Also, from the outset, project staff must be aware of the skills required for the post, particularly if organisational and committee skills are needed.

- The co-ordinator/SPW role should not be combined. The role of co-ordinator is a hard one given many activities spread over a wide geographical area. Ideally, the person appointed should have experience in management and either youth work or community development. There are several potential dangers with combining the roles:

  – objectivity may be difficult to maintain
  – interest in one role may become greater than interest in the other
  – can be taken over by the role one prefers.

These were particular difficulties with this project. One patch benefited from the combined role, but workers in the other patch felt excluded. Also a co-ordinator should not be the minute-taker at meetings because this undermines authority. The co-ordinator role should be full-time from the outset of the project as this is a critical stage in project planning.

- Considerable thought should be given to the project areas. If crime reduction is an aim, it would be better to focus on areas where this is a major issue. SACRE's knowledge of the areas was one of the reasons the patches were selected. Yet these were areas with little by way of youth crime, and while the project did find and work with young people who were disaffected with their parish council and older residents, it also worked with many young people who would fall into the category of 'nice, well mannered, middle class' young people who were not remotely at risk of social exclusion or, for instance, vulnerable to substance misuse. This rendered the aim of reducing anti-social behaviour/criminality obsolete at some interventions. The project workers could only work with the youth population available to them.

  A secondary point about the selection of these areas relates to parish council attitudes towards the project. This was interpreted as lack of interest in youth issues and in some cases may well be correct. However, it could also be the case that, as many of the parishes simply had no problems with young people in their communities, they felt no need to become involved in a project that had reducing anti-social behaviour as an aim. Several parishes declined interviews with the evaluators on these grounds.

- If the volunteer approach is taken – that is, no referrals, it is unlikely that the 'harder edged' youth are going to take part. The only 'failure' the mobile had was with a group such as this. Also, geography becomes important. Careful consideration needs to be given as to how wide an area can be covered to look for volunteers before the energy of the project is dissipated.

- The 'bottom up' model came from the project workers and while the AG made comments from time to time about whether this was appropriate, nothing was done to try to alter the model. The project workers themselves were wedded to this model, but they may have been mistaken in this instance. For example, it was almost an ideological stance with the project workers that it would take until the third year of the project to form youth fora, as the idea would need to be built up to with young people. However, in their final evaluation interviews several young people, when asked, stated that they would have been quite happy for the project workers to have suggested forming youth fora from the outset of the project. Two rather wryly made the observation that, had this happened, they would be much further on than they are now, and several expressed the view that the only way young people would have a 'serious' voice in their community was through something as formal as a properly constituted youth council. The lesson here is that perhaps adherence to one model, be it 'bottom up' or 'top down', is limiting. A combination of both may be the better approach. It also caused problems in another way. The notion that the ideas had to come from young people meant that if the ideas stopped coming from them the project workers withdrew on the basis that the young people were becoming too reliant on them. This did cause one or two young people to blame themselves for 'project failure'. Given that low self-esteem was identified as one of the problems rural youth was facing, it is difficult to see how the project helped empower young people in these instances.

- The way the patches were set up was crucial. This project was virtually two different projects; certainly this is how it felt to the project workers. One patch had the advantages of the mobile and the co-ordinator as SPW. The other project workers had no base, with no venues undercover to meet new contacts in some villages. If they had wanted to increase young people's access to facilities they would have needed to use their own cars, which was impractical and had insurance implications. Also, as one put it "what were we supposed to do if five young people turned up?" Why the patches were set up in such a way remains something of a mystery. Interview data show that noone can offer any explanation as to how this came about. However, the mobile was only allowed to operate in one patch because it was part funded by that patch's district council.

- Rural community projects need to engage with local adult decision-makers because they are such an integral part of village life. Rural youth empowerment needs their support. The successful youth fora have come about in villages where councils were receptive to the idea. Parish councils, whilst important, are not the only local decision-makers. If they show no interest others should be sought out, such as community councils and village hall committees. This project struggled to engage the interest of most of the parish councils for three years. It could perhaps have tried these other civic structures in the second year. Evaluation interviews indicate that these sources would have been more forthcoming. Several councillors also made the point that parish council work is tedious and young people could soon tire of involvement with it. It was felt that community councils and/or village hall committees might be a more interesting first step for rural youth representation.

- Whilst transport issues were obviously beyond the remit of the project, they are nonetheless critical factors and cannot pass without comment. It is well known that there is a need for affordable, regular rural bus services which also offer some late night services to enable young people to use evening facilities in the closest towns. The comments from our interviewees endorse that view. Poor public transport is an issue which affects the whole population, not just young people and, whilst rural car ownership is high, the groups with the least access to cars are elderly and young people. The view was expressed that rural public transport should be seen, in part, as a social service and funded accordingly.

Given the project difficulties: a lack of shared clarity on project aims, on-going management hiatus, an inexperienced co-ordinator, a weak AG, project staff problems and changes, underestimation of the time needed and difficulty in finding young people and poorly thought through geography, the project has done well to achieve what it has. This, to a large extent, is due to the hard work and commitment of some of the project workers.

6.

6.

Case studies

Case Study One

Angela is 15 years old and hopes to go to college when she leaves school. She lives in owner occupied housing with her parents and one younger sibling. Both parents are in employment. There is little youth provision in her village other than a youth club which is run by one of the SACRE/HO project workers in her main employment as a Community Education Youth Worker. The intervention Angela was involved in is an on-going multi-agency activity which aims to promote citizenship by involving young people in voluntary work which will benefit others in the community. Angela was engaged in a 'Changing Rooms' project which entailed a group of six young people raising the money for and then carrying out the decorating of a local centre used by, amongst others, those excluded from school and people with disabilities. At the time of writing the decorating project was successfully completed and a further project is at the planning stage.

Angela heard about the project at her village youth club. She was attracted to it because it offered a range of voluntary activities with a certificate upon completion. The idea of a certificate showing she had ability in different areas greatly appealed to her (and her friends). She has enjoyed the work enormously and particularly liked the way the young people were involved in all the decision-making. Her greatest personal satisfaction has come from knowing "they made people happy" by transforming their dingy centre. Her confidence has also increased as she now realises she has ability. The next activity is the setting up of a babysitting club. This will mean learning about "first aid and stuff". Angela hopes to be a nursery nurse so she is very excited at the prospect of the babysitting club. She feels this part of the project will be of great help to her as well as helping others.

Case Study Two

Carl is 22 years old. He has catering qualifications and works in a local pub. He lives with his parents in rented LA housing. He is planning to be a pub manager. Carl was the oldest young person involved in the project. He was part of the 'shop front hangers out' group which had occasional brushes with police and older adults over noise. He frequented the local pubs as he "didn't want to drink in the streets".

He became involved with the project when the project workers came to the youth club where he was a helper. He had already realised the club was not age appropriate for many young people and he and some friends had ideas about providing a place for them so they would not end up as 'street hangers out.' He was drawn to the project because it looked as if it could help them bring the ideas to fruition without involving "authority structures and hassling by adults".

He was left deeply disillusioned by the project. He and his friends had several sessions with project workers planning how to turn the ideas into something concrete; then the project workers just stopped coming. He left messages but never received a reply. He feels the project was no help at all in his village. Indeed, he believes it was damaging. Young people were let down yet again by adults and it has hardened his view that no one does anything for young people. He also expressed his concerns that alcohol and drug use was increasing in the village with a consequent increase in violence. He believes the only way youth will obtain anything is to have something as formal as a youth council so that they will be taken seriously.

Case Study Three

Peter is 15 years old and wants to be a mechanic when he leaves school. He lives in rented LA accommodation with his parents and three younger siblings. His father is in employment. The village is remote and has no provision for young people of his age other than the recreation ground. He and his friends felt they were watched when playing there and adults have tried to prevent them from playing football. The parish council in Peter's own village remained aloof from the project. Peter and his friends walk to the next village to use the pub and youth club there and regard this village as part of their community, having given up on their own village. His positive comments regarding parish councillors therefore relate to the adjacent village parish council.

His initial contact with the project came when the youth workers visited his school. He was drawn by the idea of young people having a voice in their community. Peter has had sustained engagement with the project over its three- year life. On a personal level he found the mobile to be particularly effective as it was "somewhere to go" and he received advice on many issues, including careers and health information. He was also involved in making the drug awareness raising posters which adorned the mobile. He particularly appreciated the relaxed style of the youth workers whom he felt "didn't talk to you like teachers do, but you were still learning things from them".

Peter has gained a lot from the project. Prior to it he hung around the bus stop with a group which was engaged in minor anti-social behaviour such as urinating and smoking. He is now a committee member of a youth forum in the adjacent village which has been formed as a result of the project and believes that the forum has had a big impact on the village. His greatest personal satisfaction has been his involvement in raising money for an adventure playground for younger children. He feels he has much more confidence around adults now and has a clearer understanding of how a village and its local civic structures operate. His views of parish councillors have moderated as a result of working with some "who were interested in us. They turned out to be OK". However, he does feel that it has been a very slow process to arrive at this point and, if the project had mooted the idea of a youth forum from the onset, they could be "a lot further on now".

Case Study Four

Mary is 18 years old and is in the 6th form at school taking a course in Advanced Social Studies. She would like to be a teacher. She lives in owner occupied housing with her parents and two younger siblings. Her mother is in employment and her father is unemployed. Prior to the project there was little youth provision in the village. She described the main youth activity as "roaming the street or going round friends, but some parents were getting annoyed with this, or sitting in the park in the freezing cold and under the slide when it rained." She wished to set up a youth club but had no idea of how to do so.

She was drawn to the project when the project workers gave a presentation at her school. She is very grateful to the project for assisting her and her friends to set up the village youth club, of which she became secretary of the management committee. She has enjoyed the responsibility this role has given her, which also included fund raising. With adults, they have successfully raised hundreds of pounds. Her greatest personal satisfaction came from "going-face-to face with the community committee. They had to listen to us because we were a formal committee ourselves and they did eventually take us seriously". The whole experience has given her more confidence; she can now speak in front of people whereas before she found it embarrassing. Mary also became a voice for the project in some ways as she attended a multi-village parish council workshop, and spoke publicly to parish councillors on how young people working with the Community Council and adults in the community had successfully set up the youth club in her village. As a result of her work for the youth club she was offered a place on the Community Council. Due to ill-health and exams she has not taken up the offer yet but does intend to do so. She also intends to become a parish councillor should the opportunity arrive.

33

The youth club ran for about two years but at the time of writing it has closed due to lack of parental support (adults have to be on the premises). However, Mary (and her friends) are determined to reinstate it.

Case Study Five

Carol is 14 years old and hopes to work with children when she leaves school. She lives with her parents and four siblings in rented LA housing. Both parents are in employment. Carol lives in the same village as Peter (Case Study Three) and, like him, uses the youth club and pub in the adjacent village and regards this as her community.

She heard about the project from friends who told her about the mobile. Initially she was too shy to go on board, getting as far as the door one day and then turning back. She continued to hear good things about it and eventually plucked up the confidence to go on board when it parked in the local pub car park. There had been a very unpleasant altercation in the village between an adult and a young person resulting in young people asking the project to help them write to the parish council about their concerns regarding a lack of voice for their age group. The initial session she attended in the mobile was the one during which the letter was composed.

She is now co-secretary (in conjunction with an adult) of the youth forum which has formed in this village as a result of the project. She is finding this very hard work but enjoying it. As secretary she has had a great deal of responsibility as the youth forum has raised hundreds of pounds for village youth facilities, and she has also been responsible for all the correspondence dealing with this. She feels that young people definitely have a voice in this community now; adults approach her in the street and ask how the youth forum is going. There is now a better understanding between adults and young people and she feels that her own understanding of village life has widened enormously. Prior to the project she felt parish councillors were "a bunch of snobs". Now that she works alongside them she has discovered they are "helpful, friendly and pleasant" and realises the difficulties which parish councils face. On a personal level her confidence is much improved and she has developed team-working skills.

Case Study Six

Penny is 17 years old and taking a NVQ in Administration. She lives at home with her parents and three siblings in owner occupied housing. Her parents are self-employed. There are no youth facilities in Penny's village and "going round friends" and "hanging around" the bus shelter are the main activities.

She heard about the mobile from friends and became involved when she heard the project workers "were not like teachers". Penny does not think the project has had any lasting impact in her village, mainly because it came at a time when some young people were too young to be interested and others were too old and about to move on. The mobile came to her village weekly at first but, due in her view to the apathy of the young people, it then came only during the holidays and finally ceased altogether. She attended every session. She received career advice and had several useful discussions with the project workers on topics she felt she could not discuss with teachers. She believes many parents were delighted to see the mobile in their village as it provided somewhere for the young people to go other than to each others' houses and gave the parents a bit of a rest from this.

Penny wanted to become a youth liaison person for the parish council as she feels it is important for young people to have a voice. The project tried to help her achieve this ambition specifically by helping her to compose a letter to the parish council outlining the proposal. The parish council response to the project workers was very negative and she personally never received a reply from the parish council. She would still like to be the liaison person for young people but does not hold out much hope.

The names of the above have been changed for reasons of confidentiality.

The Mobile

A customised motor home was equipped with a computer and a camcorder. The mobile travelled to remove villages at pre-arranged times. Young people could go on board, make hot drinks, discuss concerns, issues and needs (both personal and general) and receive help and advice. The computer was logged into the National Youth Agency database, giving young people access to a range of information. The mobile also carried leaflets on youth health issues. The camcorder was used to help young people develop new skills and to produce snapshots of village life.

Appendix B

The villages: a profile

Sixteen Suffolk villages were initially involved in this project, reduced to 13 in the final year. These fall into two Districts: Suffolk Coastal District Council and St Edmundsbury Borough Council.

The villages were:

Suffolk Coastal District Council: Alderton, Bawdsey, Eyke, Hollesley, Otley, Rendlesham, Ufford.

St Edmundsbury Borough Council: Chedburgh, Clare, Hundon, Kedington, Stansfield, Stradishall.

Suffolk Coastal – Background

Geographically, Suffolk Coastal District covers an area of 88,938 hectares and is located on the east coast of Britain to the north and east of Ipswich, the county town of Suffolk. The District has a population of 121,200 and is largely rural in character. There are many villages scattered throughout the District and a number of small towns. Much of the area is designated an Area of Outstanding Natural Beauty. Part of the area qualifies under EU Objective 5b status and also Suffolk Rural Development support.

St Edmundsbury – Background

St Edmundsbury covers an area of 655,696 hectares and the area profile is largely similar to Suffolk Coastal, except that it is inland. The principal town is Bury St Edmunds with a large industrial conurbation and two further industrial towns, Thetford and Haverhill. Surrounding these towns, and in the areas where the project was located, there are a number of remote, picturesque villages.

These data were provided by Suffolk County Council, Environment & Transport – Policy Division.

RENDLESHAM PATCH: Part of Suffolk Coastal District Council

	Total aged over 16		Economically active TOTAL		Employees Full Time		Employees Part Time		Self Employed		On Govt Scheme		Unemployed		Economically inactive Total	
	m	f	m	f	m	f	m	f	m	f	m	f	m	f	m	f
Alderton	149	152	114	65	75	30	5	27	19	1	4	1	11	6	35	87
Bawdsey	101	100	74	49	49	16	4	19	15	8	4	2	2	4	27	31
Eyke	134	138	97	77	71	34	2	29	17	11	3	1	4	2	37	61
Hollesley	523	377	304	192	237	87	11	80	38	7	9	5	9	13	219	185
Otley	263	253	201	122	130	55	3	55	53	9	3	0	12	3	62	131
Ufford	316	324	229	140	143	67	7	50	64	67	1	1	14	5	87	184
Sub-total	1486	1344	1019	645	705	289	32	260	206	53	24	10	52	33	467	699
Rendlesham	555	583	531	304	438	196	9	75	13	6	65	20	6	7	24	279

Rendlesham is an RAF base. The statistics are erratic and not included in this chart.

CLARE PATCH: Part of St Edmundsbury District Council

	Total aged over 16		Economically active TOTAL		Employees Full Time		Employees Part Time		Self Employed		On Govt Scheme		Unemployed		Economically inactive Total	
	m	f	m	f	m	f	m	f	m	f	m	f	m	f	m	f
Chedburgh	180	171	138	88	96	44	4	33	34	8	0	0	4	3	42	83
Clare	773	828	559	375	376	170	19	146	132	44	0	4	32	11	214	453
Hundon	851	416	416	202	237	105	18	66	86	21	12	0	63	10	435	214
Kedington	716	744	519	386	374	206	9	138	107	24	3	5	26	13	197	358
Stansfield	125	133	89	60	39	22	2	26	37	12	0	0	11	0	36	73
Stradishall	183	163	163	110	129	57	0	39	24	8	3	0	7	6	20	53
Sub-total	2826	2455	1884	1221	1251	604	52	448	420	117	18	9	143	43	944	1234
TOTAL:	4314	3799	2903	1866	1956	893	84	708	626	170	42	19	195	76	1411	1933
			100%	100%	67%	48%	29%	38%	21.5%	9%	1.5%	1%	3%	4%	32%	51%

According to SCC because of sampling, these statistics should be interpreted with caution.

Appendix D

DWELLINGS: NUMBER AND TENURE (based on 1991 Census)

RENDLESHAM PATCH: Part of Suffolk Coastal District Council

	Total dwell. Stock	With Residents	Vacant	Not used as Main Res	Owner Occ.	Private rental (inc. Housing Assoc)	Local Authority
Alderton	191	145	28	20	77	33	36
Bawdsey	151	101	20	31	66	33	0
Eyke	142	133	7	0	82	32	20
Hollesley	416	375	22	15	253	85	39
Otley	255	239	13	1	191	17	24
Ufford	343	318	15	7	240	37	44
Sub-total	1498	1311	105	74	909	237	163
Rendlesham	568	545	21	2	29	517	4

Rendlesham is a former USA military base. The statistics are erratic and are not included in the totals.

CLARE PATCH: Part of St Edmundsbury District Council

Chedburgh	178	168	8	1	136	11	19
Clare	851	796	42	18	499	111	180
Hundon	449	408	22	13	345	34	35
Kedington	673	626	45	3	504	60	59
Stansfield	156	132	6	17	89	20	19
Stradishall	171	154	12	3	94	37	22
Sub-totals:	2478	2284	135	55	1667	273	334
TOTAL	3976	3595	240	129	2576	510	497
	100%	90.40%	6%	3.25%	65%	12.80%	12.50%

POPULATION ESTIMATES (based on 1991 Census)

	1997[1]	1991	Male	Female	Pensioners In H/Holds	Age 5-15	Range 16/17	18-29
RENDLESHAM PATCH: Part of Suffolk Coastal District Council								
Alderton	420	380	181	192	65	48	13	72
Bawdsey	250	260	124	129	53	40	5	33
Eyke	350	370	178	181	61	68	8	40
Hollesley	1280	1160	659	476	148	159	25	279
Otley	680	680	346	320	111	118	23	88
Ufford	820	790	382	389	186	89	17	111
Sub-total:	3800	3640	1870	1687	624	522	91	623
Rendlesham[2]	1460	2620	974	953	29	442	35	499
CLARE PATCH: Part of St Edmundsbury District Council								
Chedburgh	570	450	232	209	81	55	15	66
Clare	2030	2000	964	1012	473	299	58	259
Hundon	1450	1480	958	499	211	125	33	317
Kedington	1790	1810	848	932	258	210	61	265
Stansfield	200	200	169	152	73	40	8	38
Stradishall	350	440	230	208	30	60	12	110
Sub-total:	6390	6380	3401	3012	1126	789	187	1055
TOTAL:	10190	10020	5271	4699	1750	1311	278	1678

1 1977 update provided by Suffolk County Council
2 Rendlesham is former USA military base

Appendix F

ALL CRIMINAL DAMAGE – 1997 (Notifiable Offences Recorded by Police)

	No. of cases	Population	Rate per 100,000
Clare Patch*	28	6,390	438
Rendlesham Patch*	15	2,340	641
Project as a whole*	43	8,730	493
England & Wales **	877,042	50 m	1,754

** Ref 1997 Criminal Statistics for England and Wales Cm4162
* This is unaudited data and may differ from official statistics
NB: The figures for the village of Rendlesham have been excluded because this village is a former USA military base and the vacated housing stock was used by councils in other parts of the country. Consequently this village has a cosmopolitan population and has the characteristics of a town rather than a village. For that reason its figures are anomalous.

Advisory Group Members at Outset of Project

Head of Development (Community & Policy), Suffolk ACRE

Co-ordinator, Suffolk ACRE

Regional Development Agency Field Officer, Suffolk County Council

County Co-ordinator, Suffolk Crime Reduction

Suffolk Constabulary

Health Promotion, Suffolk Health Authority

Community Education Development Officer

Town Councillor, Saxmundham

Town Councillor, Clare

PDU (two members)

Appendix H

Interventions

Activity	Access to facilities	Citizenship	Reducing anti-social behaviour	Outcome
Residentials 1 & 2	yes	yes	n/a	two residentials completed but no follow-up
Europe:Sonenburg & Belgium	n/a	yes	n/a	Sonenburg cancelled as being too ambitious. Eyke successful outcome.
Befriending Scheme	x	x	x	No outcome.
Urban visit/Birmingham	x	x	x	No outcome. Cancelled by Birmingham.
Peer Education	n/a	yes	yes	Several successful outcomes.
Mobile	yes	yes	yes	Successfully engaged with young people throughout the project.
Youth Parish Council/Forum	yes	yes	yes	Three set up during project. One set up post project.
Youth N/hood Watch	x	x	x	No outcome. Cancelled with AG agreement because difficult to obtain an adult interest. NHW too difficult with young people.
Parish Council Seminar	n/a	n/a	n/a	Altered to PC workshop in year three.
Training	n/a	yes	yes	Young people successfully completed course.
Needs Survey High School	n/a	n/a	n/a	Findings fed into project.
Pocket Park	x	x	x	No outcome. No interest from young people.
Minibus Outings	x	x	x	Young people declined this service.
Sports Sessions	x	x	x	No outcome. No attenders for the swimming and inter-agency football due to peer group pressure.
PR Work	n/a	n/a	n/a	No outcome. Youth workers not skilled in PR.
Peer Support	n/a	n/a	n/a	Informal. Ongoing throughout the project.

Community leader comments

One civic leader wished the following comments to be drawn to the attention of the Home Office and/or any other relevant department.

- Young people already face considerable difficulties with their parish councils regarding accessing green/recreation areas of their villages. This situation is going to worsen because parish councils are to be held responsible for, and liable to, prosecution regarding any accidents on these grounds.

- On some recreation grounds there is little more than portable goal posts and even this sparse resource is likely to be removed due to the publicity surrounding the collapsing of this type of goal post.

This interviewee felt strongly that these issues needed addressing via some integrated policy for rural youth which should come from central government.

Appendix J

Other agency contacts

As well as the involvement of other agencies in some of the project interventions, the co-ordinator and the other project workers also attended other agency meetings, for example:

- Suffolk Careers Service

- Suffolk Council for Voluntary Organisations

- Suffolk's Drug Action Team

- Suffolk Association of Youth

- Suffolk Youth Partnership

Criminality/anti-social behaviour in rural areas

A supplementary report

Introduction

This report came about as a result of the external evaluation of the *Empowering Young People in Rural Suffolk* project, which was primarily funded by the Home Office and managed by Suffolk Action with Communities in Rural England (SACRE). The aim of that project was to improve access to facilities for young people, to engage them in citizenship within their communities and to reduce criminality: the overall objective was to establish a community where young people have a sense of 'ownership' and self worth, in which criminality does not have an opportunity to take hold. It was already known that there is a comparatively low level of criminality among young people in rural areas and this has been confirmed recently by Mirrlees-Black (1998). Nevertheless, from the perspective of those who reside in rural areas, the level of anti-social behaviour in some villages is significant and therefore should not be ignored and there is some criminality. Of course, what is considered anti-social is, to some extent, subjective but there seems to be some consensus as to how this is interpreted, particularly in villages.

The method of evaluation for the SACRE project was qualitative and involved interviewing local councillors, business representatives and young people involved in the project. They were asked about the level of criminality in their villages and their views on why incidents of criminality are low in these communities. Separate from the SACRE project, unstructured interviews were carried out with representatives of the police and the Youth Offending Team Service to add a wider perspective for the purpose of this report. However, it should be remembered that this is an additional report to the main SACRE report which had a different remit and, as such, the comments should be seen as valid but not necessarily conclusive or generalisable

Suffolk is predominantly rural, its coast and heaths are AONB (Areas of Outstanding Natural Beauty). The majority of the county is a mix of less densely populated suburban areas (hereafter referred to as LDPSAs) and extreme rurality. In common with many other rural areas, it has been subject to the population changes which started in the 1970s, with many people retiring to its 'picture postcard' villages and younger newcomers leaving the 'rat race'. During the decade 1971-81 it experienced high levels of population changes. Also in common with other rural areas, it suffered public transport reduction, loss of shops and village schools.

Whilst the *focus* of this report is criminality and anti-social behaviour, it must be read in the context of the incidents discussed taking place over a period of years and in some villages there were no problems at all. The overall low crime rate is evidenced by an example of criminal damage statistics: in 1997 the figures for 12 villages involved in the SACRE report ranged from a high of 13 to a low of zero, with the average figure being three to four incidents .

These figures are for the whole population, that is, they include adult offenders and not just young people.

With these caveats in mind the report can be used to support the few findings on this topic from other published sources and could be used to formulate further research in this substantive area.

Farrington (1996) comments that research should be concerned with protective as well as risk factors. Farrington notes the major risk factors, as intervening variables, for youth crime as:

- Low income and poor housing
- Living in deteriorated inner city areas
- A high degree of impulsiveness and hyperactivity
- Low intelligence and low school attainment
- Poor parental supervision and harsh and erratic discipline
- Parental conflict and broken families.

The protective factors are:

- Effective supervision provided by the young person's family
- Families with pro-social beliefs
- The family's interest in their child's education.

This report looks at some of the reasons for the low level of criminality/anti-social behaviour, and how the situation in villages relates to the risk and protective factors outlined in the literature.

The British Crime Survey (1996) defines 'rural' as villages and LDPSAs. The data referred to in this report have mainly been collected in villages but there is some reference to the LDPSAs. The term 'urban areas' refers to urban and inner city areas. The following section of this report gives a picture of criminality/anti-social behaviour provided by the interview data.

Picture of criminality/anti-social behaviour

An impression has been built up of anti-social behaviour among young people in some villages. Many village residents are retired and there are few young people. These young people lack facilities and there is a paucity of transport to take them to facilities in nearby towns. Youth work can be non-existent. The lack of facilities can lead to boredom which in turn may lead to anti-social behaviour or criminality such as substance misuse, vandalism and under age driving. A recent local press article supports this description of rural village life (Eastern Daily Press 9.12.99. P.iii). To quote Farrington (1996, p.2) vandalism and taking vehicles (the most common types of offences in rural villages) as youth offender crimes, ... "are committed ... to relieve boredom". Young people need access to information and they need mobile provision so that they have a meeting place. Mirrlees-Black's (1998) findings on rural areas and crime show that litter and vandalism, teenagers hanging around and drug use are issues of greatest concern.

Examples of criminality

Vandalism and other anti-social behaviour

Vandalism is a problem in some villages. Where this happens it is sometimes carried out by older young people who may have been drinking excessive amounts of alcohol. Typical acts of vandalism are breaking village hall windows, lifting paving stones and removing new signs. Sometimes the young people are wrongly accused, for instance, one incident of a broken gate was accidentally done by a young child. Another incident related to young people using the churchyard gravestones as a backdrop to making shadow puppets by moonlight. Not anti-social behaviour as such, but it concerned adults in the village who considered it disrespectful.

Other problems are excessive noise caused by cars and motorbikes, petty crime such as amateurish burglaries, usually in neighbouring villages, minor graffiti and some shoplifting by younger young people; in one shop this was caused by the refusal of the shopkeeper to sell alcohol and cigarettes to under-age young people. There is some evidence that noise nuisance is increasing and generally incidents are likely to be under-reported. Very occasionally there have been more isolated serious incidents, such as holding up the village shopkeeper with a replica gun and stealing cars, the latter committed by older young people. One incident that was related happened years earlier and has entered the realms of village folklore; a mini-crime wave took place due to a very elderly shopkeeper opening all hours and falling asleep at the cash till. Once word went around people came from far and wide to shoplift. The local constabulary persuaded her to close earlier and the crime wave stopped.

Substance misuse (drug taking/smoking)

It is difficult to build up a true picture of drug taking in villages but the overall use is probably low level and usually attributed to the older young people, that is the 19 to 20 year olds, and there may be only one drug user in a village. However, it is thought that there is widespread use of soft drugs in the LDPSAs which is on the increase in line with the increase in drug and alcohol misuse nationally. There was evidence from the interviews of some peer group pressure to smoke.

Scale/fear of crime

The incidence of crime and anti-social behaviour is low but it cannot be dismissed as non-existent and therefore unimportant. It is just the scale of the problem which is different in comparison with the LDPSAs, and these areas in turn when compared with urban areas.

Although LDPSAs are termed 'rural', some of them are among the most deprived areas in the country. The same risk factors exist in these areas such as family poverty, incidences of abuse and poor infrastructure including poor housing, but there are no huge housing estates and, according to the British Crime Survey, the 'high risk' areas are the poorest council estates.

As a result of the London overspill policy in the 1960s a small village could become a LDPSA. The resulting high unemployment level has been linked to the incidence of alcohol and drug misuse. In one, probably typical, LDPSA area over half the current recorded crimes are criminal damage, which is a crime most likely to have been committed by young people.

It should be borne in mind that by definition populations are small in villages, and therefore there are proportionately fewer people to commit crimes or behave anti-socially. However, if there is an increase in the number of incidents, the impact is much more noticeable than in urban areas and although retired people's perception of crime is exaggerated, nonetheless it is a very real fear for them. As mentioned above, crime in a village can relate to one family. An example was given of a social services department relocating a few families who had 'Looked After' children to a rural locality leading to a sharp increase in the number of crimes in this particular locality. This shows up the difficulty of obtaining a true picture of events from quantitative data alone.

Problems created by young people come and go as a result of their transition to adulthood and, as one group of young people moves on, another moves into this phase. Because there are so few young people in each community, and often a whole peer group will not cause any trouble, there are lulls in anti-social activity.

Occasionally in these villages adults become aggressive to the young people who retaliate, for example, by throwing stones at the adult's window. The older young people have added to the fear of crime of older residents, who tend not to distinguish between older and younger young people. It is worth mentioning here that the fear of crime is actually largely a fear of violence (Osborne et al, 1995).

Low tolerance of young people

One of the reasons for anti-social behaviour is boredom and the lack of a sense of achievement as a result of the lack of activities. The young people start hanging around and become stuck in that way of life. According to one of the project workers the young people often become disillusioned with the lack of facilities, and lack of adult support and understanding, and turn to anti-social behaviour. Generally there is a lower level of tolerance of anti-social behaviour in rural communities than in urban centres and the police seem to be part of this culture; in fact, the police sometimes appear to over-react. An example was given by the young people of a group of them riding their motorbikes on a disused railway line; in this case the nearby residents were happy for these young people to be there because they preferred them to be safer off-road, but the police stopped them. Another group of young people mentioned that a young person, who had removed a new bank sign in the village, was taken to the police cell for a short period and later, according to them, was "sent out of the area to his Gran's". Sometimes the police may be losing an opportunity to build up better relationships with the young people.

Overall, protective factors seem to be more in evidence than risk factors and even where there are risk factors present these are sometimes ameliorated, for example, by single parents often being supported by their mothers and grandmothers living nearby.

Low Criminality

The protective factors, mentioned earlier, are all supported by the interview data.

Socio-economic conditions

Unemployment is considered a risk factor in relation to crime/criminality. The predominant type of housing in villages is owner occupied (see Appendix D in main report). This is likely to indicate that families in villages are more likely to have a higher income that those in urban areas. This in turn probably indicates a higher level of employment, a population with more skills, more education and more likelihood, therefore, of being pro-social. Generally, crime reduction is hard to sustain because the incidence of crime is related to social and economic conditions and family support (Osborne et al, 1995). In rural villages the socio-economic conditions are generally good. For instance, it is known from the British Crime Surveys for 1992, 1994 and 1996 that people who live in rural areas are more likely to be in managerial and professional employment, thereby perhaps providing more evidence to support this correlation.

A point relating to transport and employment is worth noting. An example was given to us of a young person being able to take the bus to work, but unable to make the return journey due to lack of public transport. This may be quite common. Given that unemployment is a risk factor for criminality, the importance of public transport needs considering in this light.

Sense of community

In the interviews the most common response to the reasons for low criminality was "everyone knows everyone". This is true of the police as well; in one village there was a mini drug raid by the police as they and the community knew exactly who was involved. The parents usually have control and, as mentioned earlier, they also tend to have a low level of tolerance of anti-social behaviour. The community tends to police its own area and the police appear to fit in with this local culture. Informal police warnings are very common in villages; a warning is given and the police may follow this up by informing the parents. Whilst the police are not usually on patrol in the villages there is evidence that they respond quickly when called.

Graham and Bowling (1995) comment that offending is related to less parental supervision and less home attachment, and for girls, less attachment to school. The majority of young people we interviewed felt that they and their peers had the support of their parents and overall the communities were close and friendly. The parents tended to impart a strong sense of right and wrong: Farrington (1996) also comments that young people need a basis for making moral judgements and they need to learn from those around them to be concerned for others.

Our data showed that village pubs are often the centres of the community, allowing young people in to meet there. If the parents go to the pub their sons and daughters often go with them. An example was given by one young person of making up a pub pool team with her parents and her older sister. A publican commented that young people channel their energies into the few facilities which exist. Some of the young people commented that because there are so few facilities they value them and even the incidence of vandalism is not high because there is so little to vandalise.

The school is thought to play a role in giving young people a sense of community. Although there may be evidence of some inter village and group rivalry, this is likely to be secondary to their sense of belonging to their school which may cover several villages in the catchment area. The young people often feel accepted by their community which is less likely to be the case in larger communities.

In conclusion Osborne et al (1995) refer to a programme of activities for young people with the purpose of giving them "… a strong sense of belonging to their community" which exists in rural villages. There is also reference to a 'street warden' service which a village naturally has through, to paraphrase our interviewees, "everyone knowing everyone". The family, the school and the local neighbourhood are all strong positive influences in rural villages, which supports findings that prevention programmes need to target these domains.

Space/lack of overcrowding

Overcrowded households are a risk factor for criminality among young people, although it is not known whether this is a direct influence or indirect through increased stress on the family (Farrington 1996). One of the interviewees referred to the 'Russian rat analogy'; that is, that overcrowding in urban areas leads people to turn on each other. Certainly, there are no large housing estates in villages to become centres of criminality.

Use of alcohol/drugs

Drugs are not as accessible in small communities as they are in larger ones. Rural young people in villages tend not to be streetwise and there is not too much peer pressure which is partly because there are not many peers. However, as mentioned earlier, there does appear to be a problem with alcohol misuse and older young people.

Conclusion

This report can only give a descriptive and to some extent anecdotal picture of criminality in this possibly fairly typical rural area, using the data collected, with a tentative interpretation of what lies behind this picture. Incidences of criminality/anti-social behaviour are low but the perceptions of crime are very real and there are growing tensions in some areas giving rise to some concern. However, the picture we have gained is interesting regarding protective factors and gives support to the view that these factors, when strengthened, could lead to a reduction in criminality.

References

Osborne, S. and Shaftoe, H. (1995) *Successes and failures in neighbourhood crime prevention.* Housing Research 149. Joseph Rowntree Foundation.

Farrington, D. (1996) *Understanding and preventing youth crime.* Social Policy Research 93. Joseph Rowntree Foundation.

Graham, J. and Bowling, B. (1995) *Young People and crime.* Home Office Research Study 145.

Mirrlees-Black, C. (1998) *Rural areas and crime. Findings from the British Crime Survey.* Home Office.

Utting, D. (1996) *Reducing criminality among young people: a sample of relevant programmes in the UK.* Home Office Research Study 161.

"Vandalism and crime are teenagers' escape", *Eastern Daily Press,* 9 Dec 1999.

RDS Publications

Requests for Publications

Copies of our publications and a list of those currently available may be obtained from:

> Home Office
> Research, Development and Statistics Directorate
> Communication Development Unit
> Room 275, Home Office
> 50 Queen Anne's Gate
> London SW1H 9AT
> Telephone: 020 7273 2084 (answerphone outside of office hours)
> Facsimile: 020 7222 0211
> E-mail: publications.rds@homeoffice.gsi.gov.uk

alternatively

why not visit the RDS website at
> Internet: http://www.homeoffice.gov.uk/rds/index.html

where many of our publications are available to be read on screen or downloaded for printing.